Mountains divide provinces, nowhere more dramatically than between Canterbury and Westland. Leave the reminiscently English city of Christchurch and drive across the flat alluvial Canterbury Plains where lambs are fattening for the export market. Drive to the foothills of Porter's Pass leading to the West Coast. If it is winter, youngsters will be tobogganing down snow-slopes on plastic rubbish bags, a popular Sunday's outing. In no time you are in sight of the Craigieburn Range, then on to the tiny alpine village of Arthur's Pass, in the heart of the main divide. It could be the European Alps, but the sudden drop through the rugged Otira Gorge into Westland is unmistakably New Zealand. Here moisture-laden air from the Tasman Sea drops its burden on the mountain barrier of the Southern Alps. The grass is greener, the forest lush, the rivers numerous in Westland.

All is not alpine and rural however. Within the six provinces of the South Island are several cities, but it is fair to comment they are more similar in atmosphere to large towns. Ask any South Islander and they will tell you that is the way they like it, and wish it to stay. They prefer the sparsely spread population, the wide open spaces and unspoilt places. Where else on such a small island could be found luxuriant rainforest and cascading waterfalls, mighty rivers and scenic lakes, barren hill tussock land and rolling green pastures? The contrasts are amazing. This is what South Islanders love and gain solace from. But most of all it is the mountains.

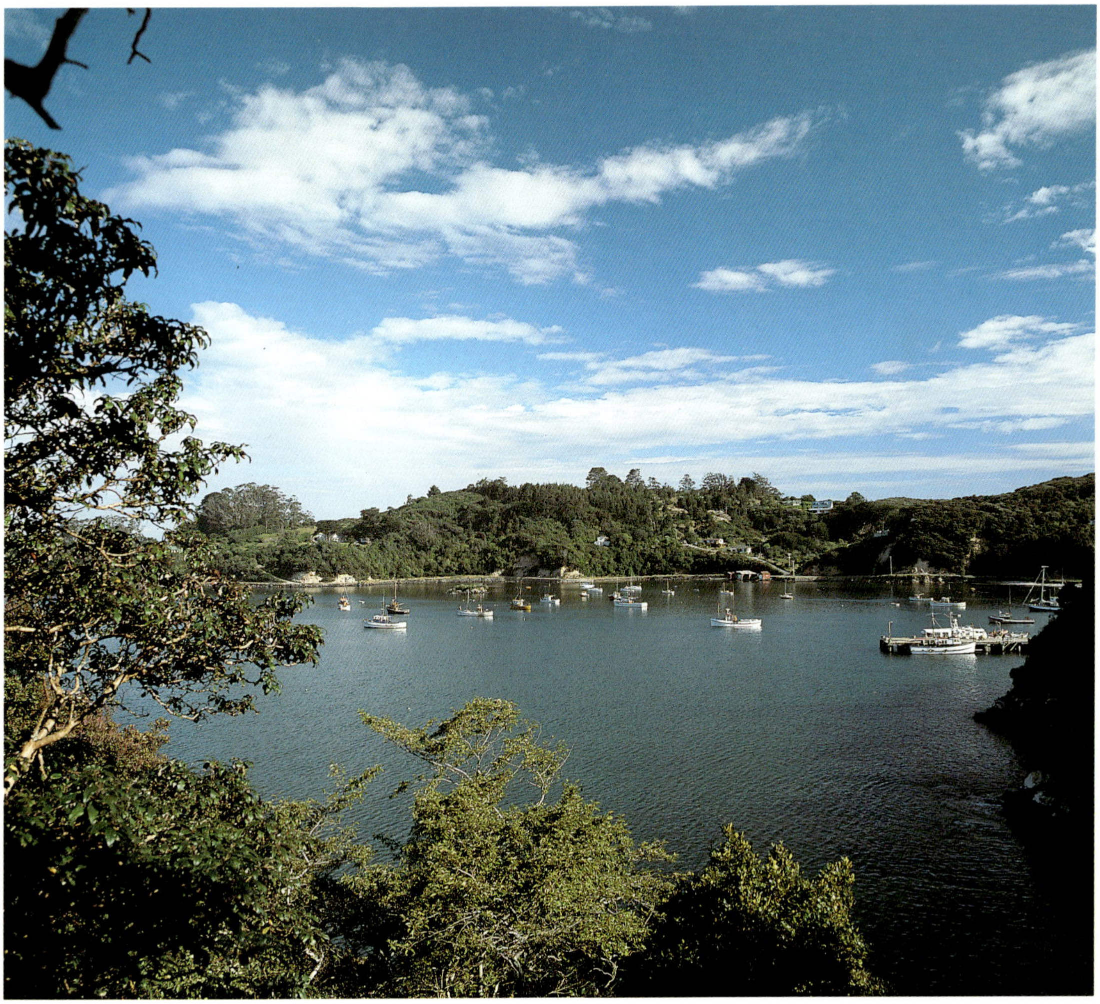

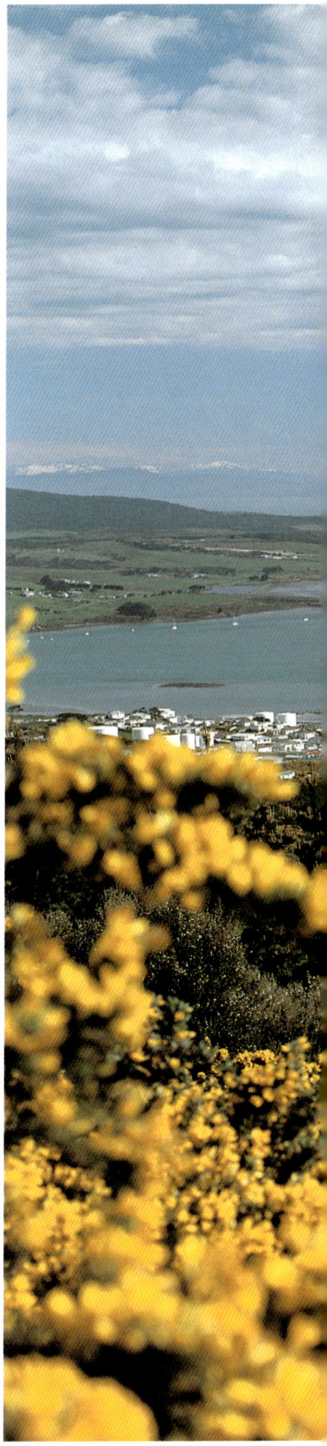

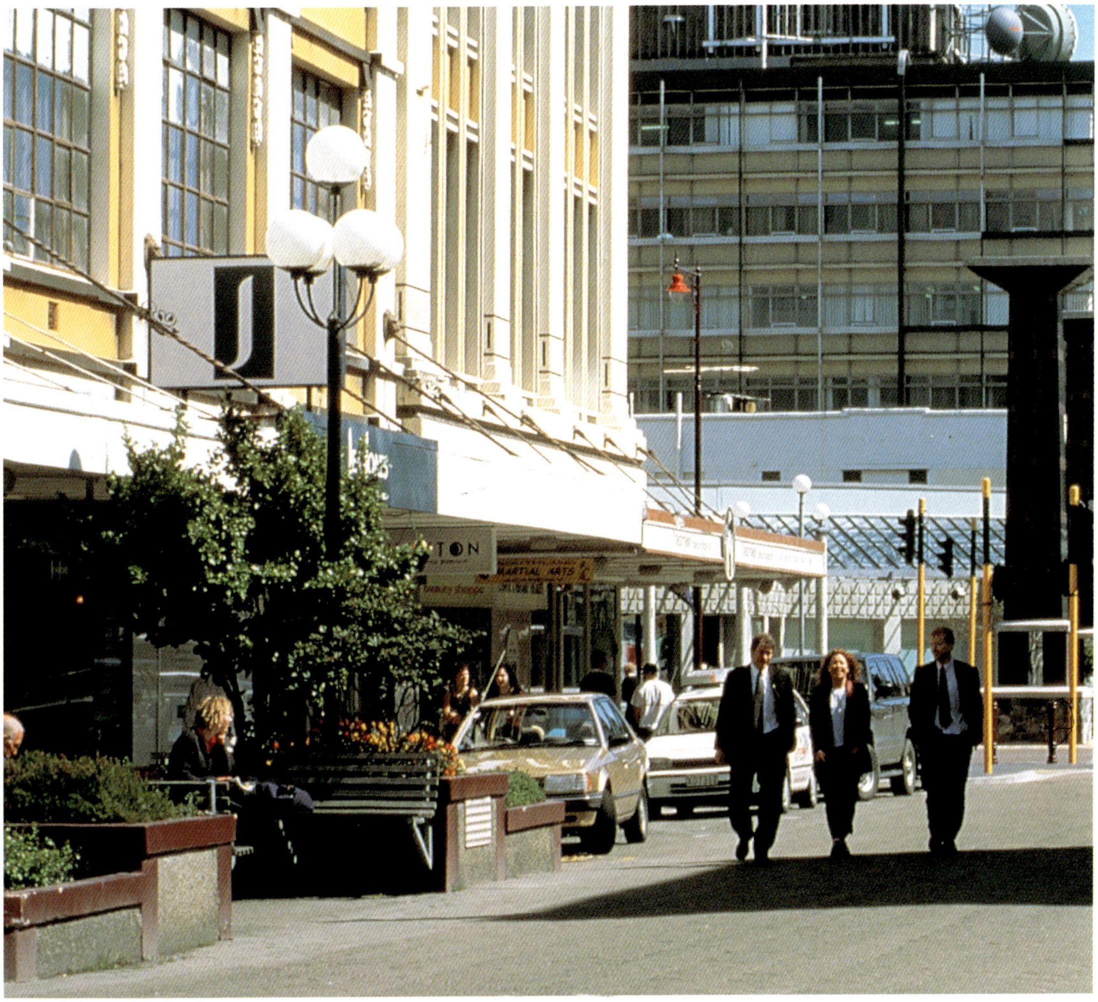
TON
MARTIAL ARTS

Left Above
The 30km of Foveaux Strait that separates Stewart Island from the South Island mainland are sufficient to make it an unspoilt haven of New Zealand bird life and scenery. Only the sandy beaches near Halfmoon Bay show any sign of habitation.

Left
Invercargill is the southernmost city of New Zealand and although not known for its highrises or population growth, can be proud of the fact that it serves one of the most productive farming communities in the country.

Above
Bluff Harbour is home port for many of the fleet that commercially fish Foveaux Strait, well known for its oyster beds. New Zealand Aluminium Smelters has its large smelter on Tiwai Point at the entrance to the Harbour. The raw materials are shipped in from Queensland, Australia, and power supplied directly from Manapouri.

Left
Tautuku Bay is a perfect crescent shaped beach ending in a small peninsula of farmland and holiday houses, or cribs as they are called in this southern part of New Zealand. It is in the Catlins District on the coastal road from Invercargill to Balclutha, one of the most scenic drives in the South Island.

Right
The Eglinton Valley is the gateway to Fiordland National Park on the Te Anau to Milford Road. From Lake Te Anau the road follows the valley floor into dense forest passing gems of small trout fishing lakes, Gunn, Fergus and tiny Lake Lochie, actually a mountain tarn with no outlet.

Below
The Fiordland National Park was included in the South-West New Zealand World Heritage Park site in 1990. Its headquarters are on the shores of Lake Te Anau, a thriving small resort which caters well for the large number of tourists who come to explore the rivers, lakes, mountains and walking tracks within the park.

Above
Mitre Peak's glacially carved cliffs rise 1692m from the deep waters of Milford Sound, making it one of the highest sea wall peaks in the world. The sound is the South Island's greatest tourist attraction and was given the title "eighth wonder of the world" by well-known author Rudyard Kipling.

Right
The Sutherland Falls, the 4th highest in the world, are on the Milford Track, the famous 55km walkway between Te Anau and Milford Sound. The surveyor Quinton MacKinnon and his companion Ernest Mitchell were the first to make the complete trip in 1888, cutting the track as they went. Donald Sutherland, after whom these falls are named, had unsuccessfully tried from the Milford side but had to retreat because of huge avalanches.

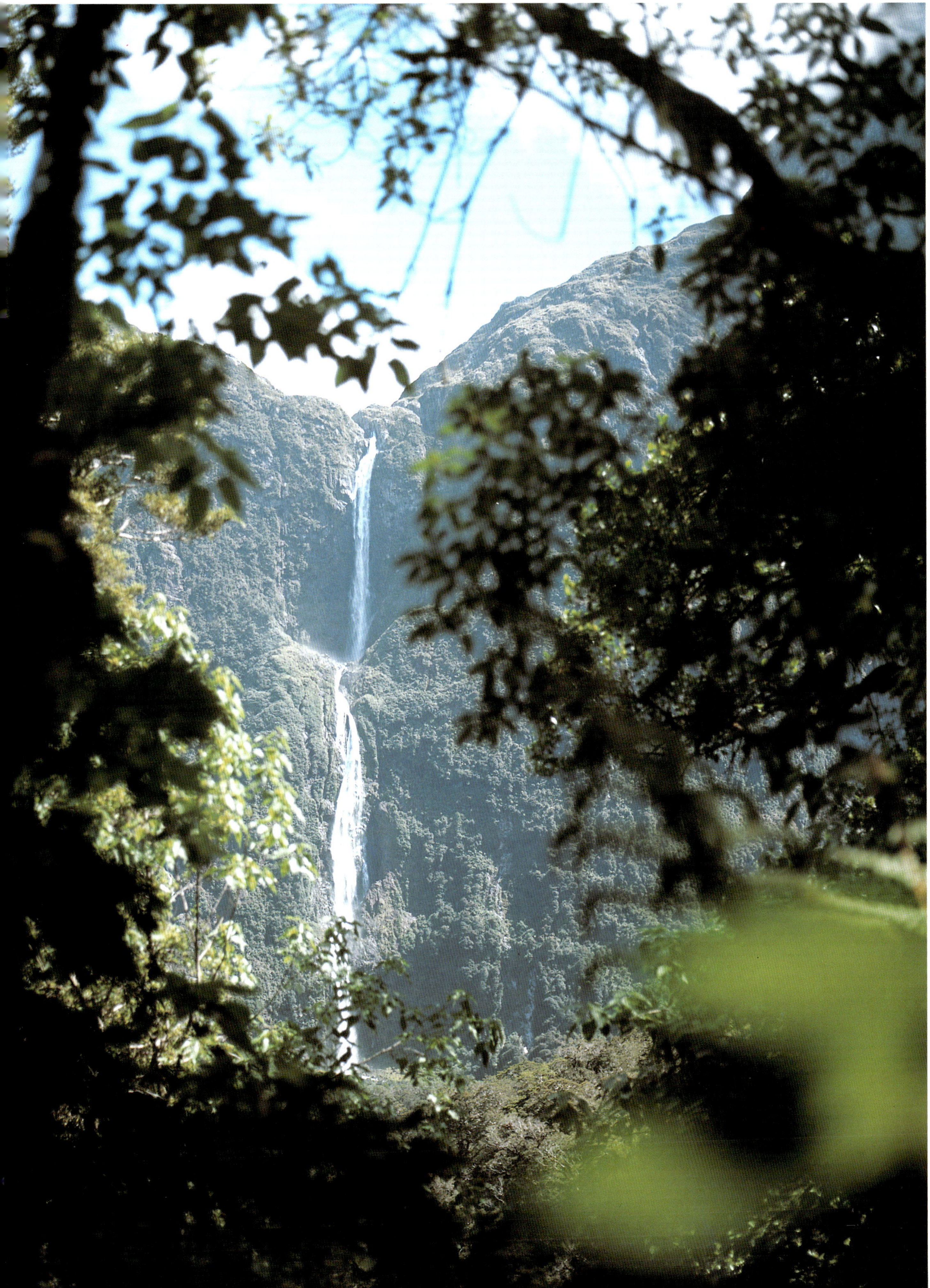

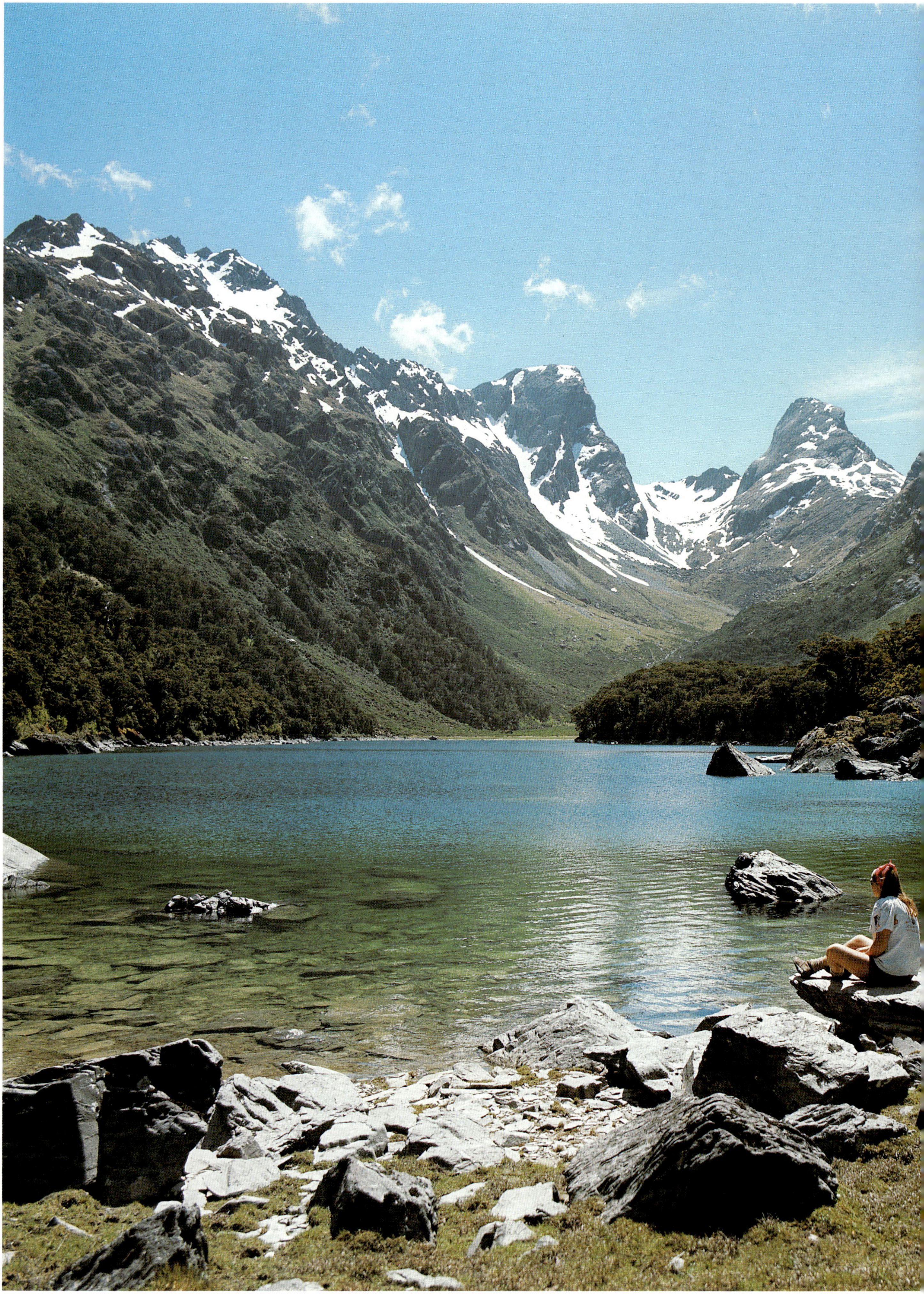

Left
The Te Anau to Milford road offers some of the most spectacular mountain scenery in the world. It passes through the Upper Hollyford Valley where there are several pretty alpine lakes. One of the most picturesque is Lake McKenzie, reached via the Routeburn Track, which has an imposing background of Mt Emily and Ocean Peak.

Above
The mountainous rock faces of the 15km long Milford Sound are covered in waterfalls after a Fiordland rain, an occurrence that on average happens 183 days in the year. To gain the full impact of the magnitude of the rock walls and the depth of the crystal clear water, it is best to take an excursion on one of the several tourist boats that travel the length of the Sound.

Above
Queenstown is the leading tourist centre of the Southern Lakes district. It nestles on Lake Wakatipu where the southern and central arms meet and is completely surrounded by mountains that can be snow covered in winter. Excursions leave from here for all the scenic and historically fascinating goldmining attractions of the district.

Left
In the early days of New Zealand's history the Queenstown district was known for its large sheep runs on the shores of Lake Wakatipu. From 1912 the TSS *Earnslaw* has been the means of communication for station families and still steams regularly up to Walter Peak and Mt Nicholas Station, only nowadays carrying sightseers instead of sheep and provisions.

Right
Queenstown is an all year round resort. During summer months people flock to enjoy the amazing variety of outdoor activities available—white water rafting, jet boating, bungy jumping or para-sailing on the lake. In winter the scenario changes to ski hats and four wheel drive vehicles as two major commercial skifields, Coronet Peak and The Remarkables are right at Queenstown's door.

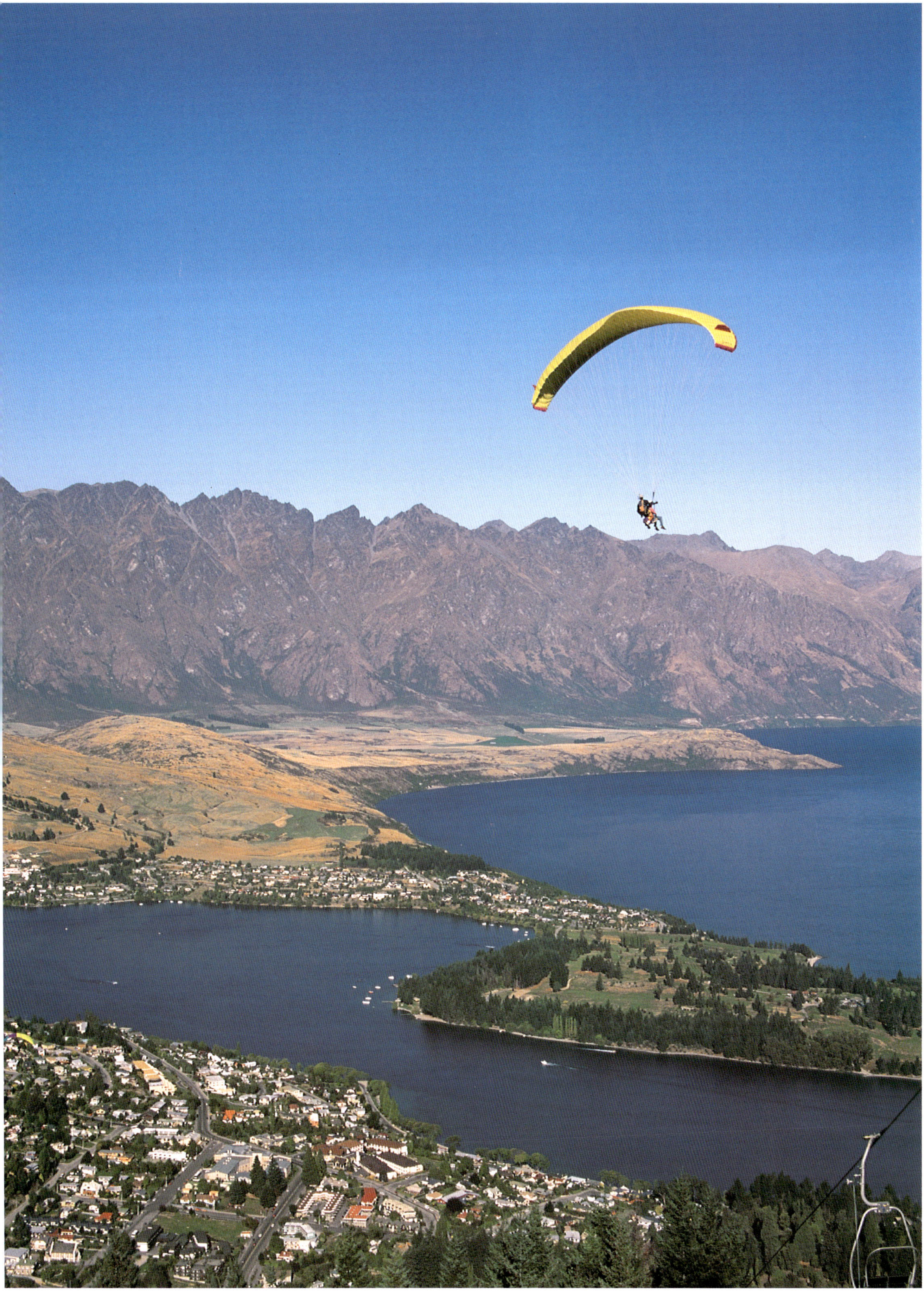

Above
Only a short drive from the cities of Invercargill and Dunedin, Queenstown has become a favourite location for retirement. It has all the necessary amenities, as well as spectacular views. This one is from the Skyline Chalet which looks out over township and lake to Kelvin Heights and the Remarkables.

Right Above
The whole of Central Otago mushroomed when gold was discovered in 1861. St Bathans was a prosperous goldboom township but now a sleepy hollow where the pub could tell of fortunes made and the nearby Blue Lake, whose crater was formed by years of excavation, of the toil it took.

Right Below
Lake Hayes is one of the smaller of Central Otago's lakes, with a delightful rural setting. It was called by the Maori, Te Wai Whaka-ata (the waters of reflection), a much more appropriate name than its English title, the misspelling of the name of its colonial discoverer, an Australian stockman Donald Hay.

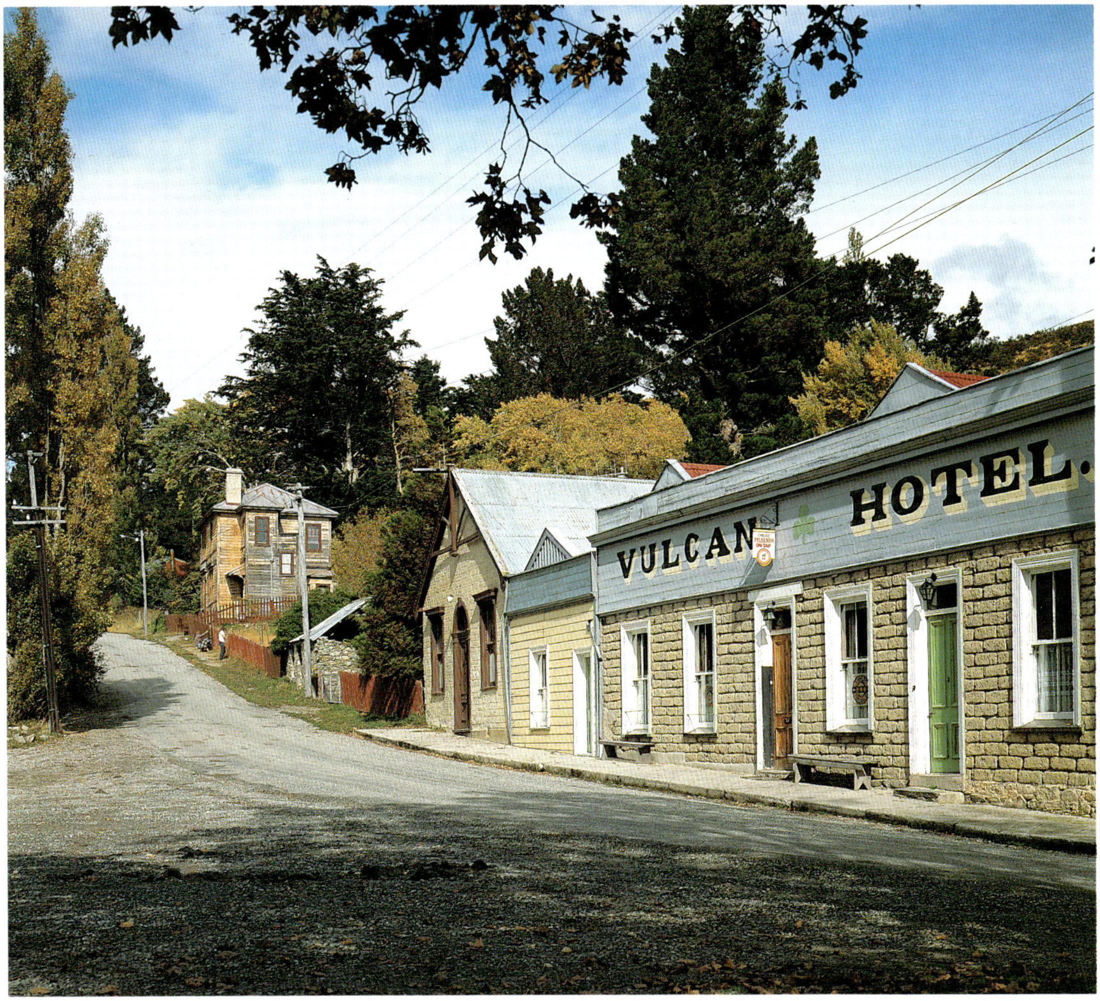
VULCAN HOTEL.

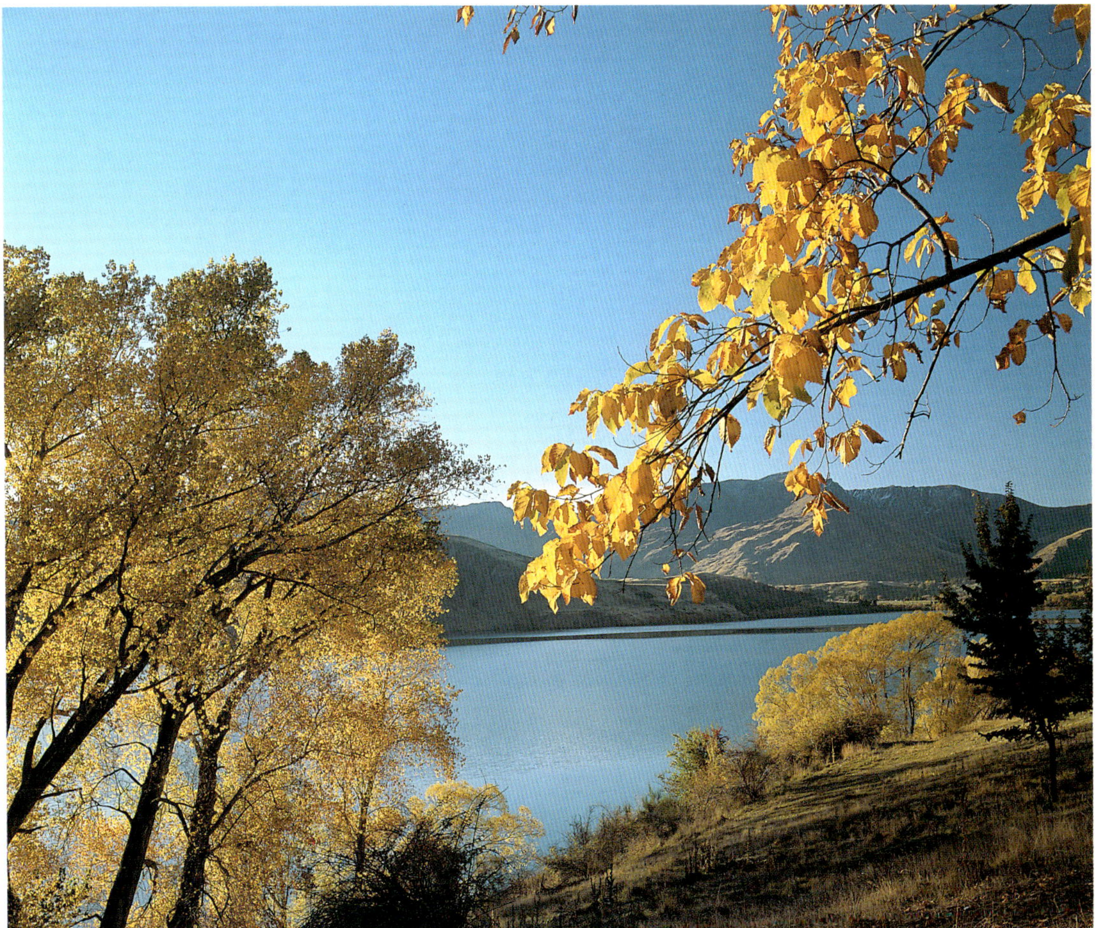

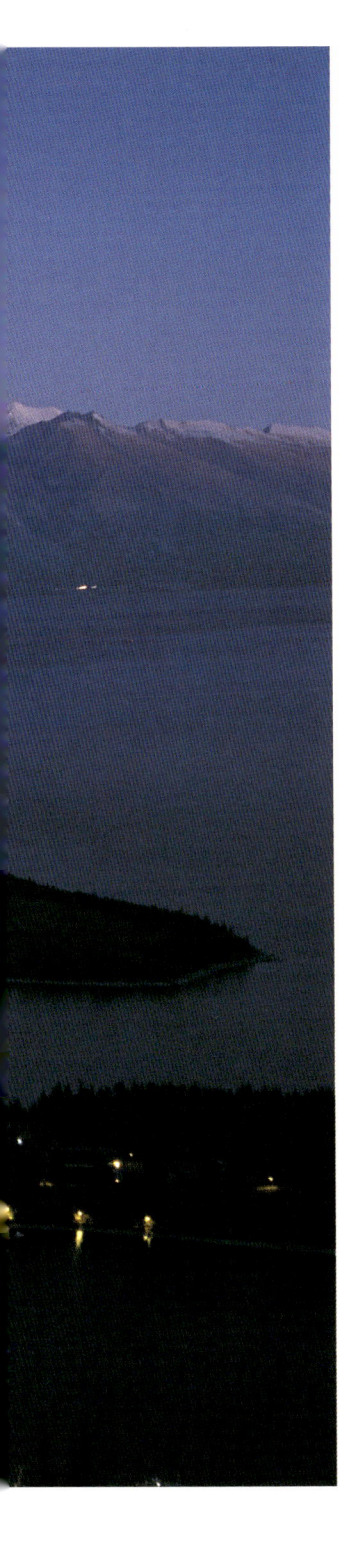

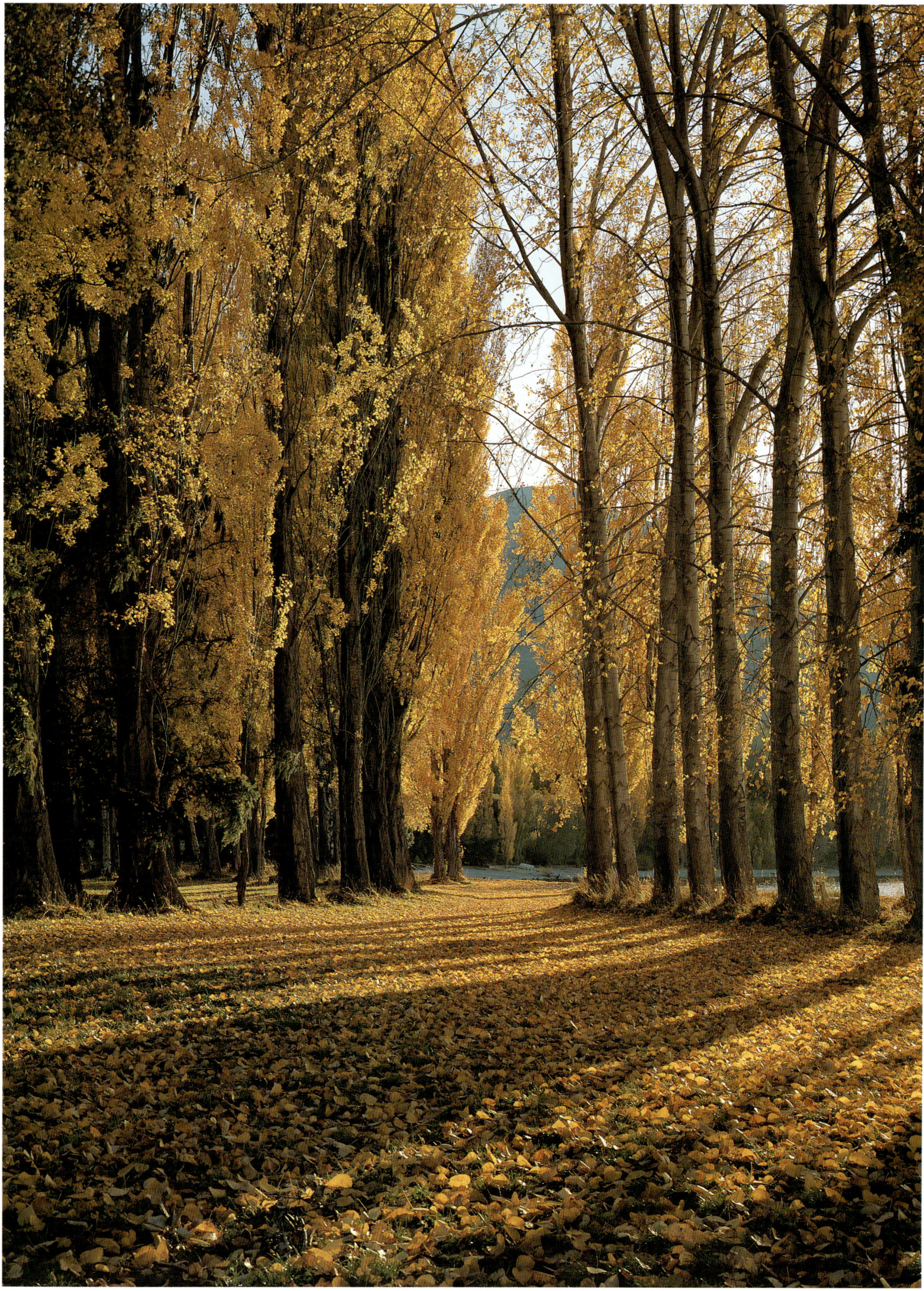

Left
For their true splendour, the Southern Lakes should be visited in autumn. Long dry summers followed by crisp frosty mornings turn the leaves of poplar and willow into a palette of assorted colour, as here along the shores of Lake Wanaka.

Below
Wanaka has always been a sheep farming district, but is also gateway to the Aspiring National Park and two of the South Island's most popular skifields, Cardrona and Treble Cone. Because of the dual role Wanaka has a more homely rural charm than its competitor resort, Queenstown.

Above
There are many interesting historic buildings throughout the South Island, reminders of an interesting colonial past. This is the stone woolshed at Morven Hills Station, still in use today. Before the days of electricity 20 or 30 shearers would hand clip up to 3,000 sheep a day in sheds such as this.

Right
The McKenzie Country, a huge basin of high country grassland in South Canterbury, has a remoteness and grandeur all its own. The harshness of the landscape is broken by the turquoise waters of Lake Tekapo, fed by glaciers deep in the Main Divide of the Southern Alps.

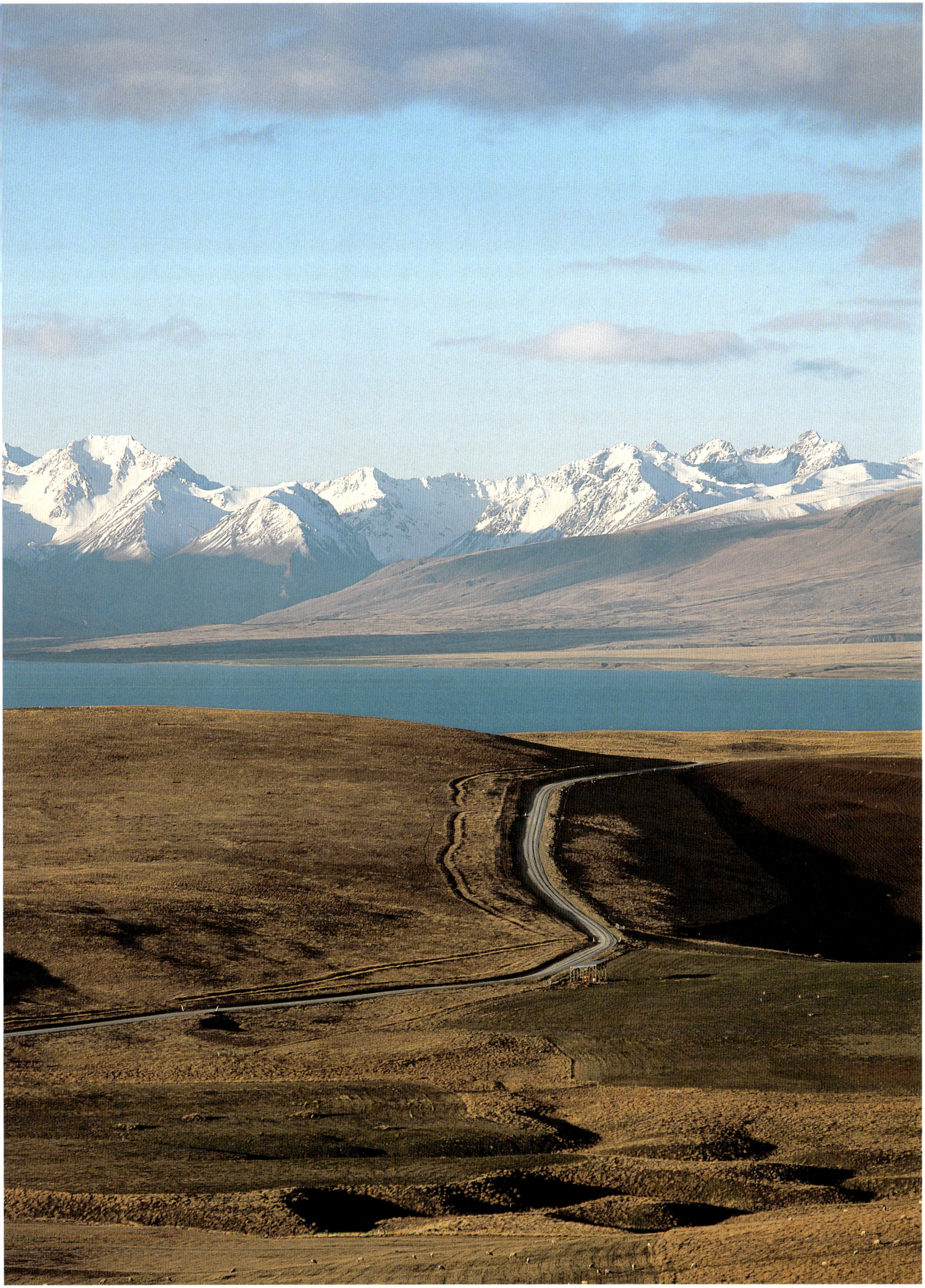

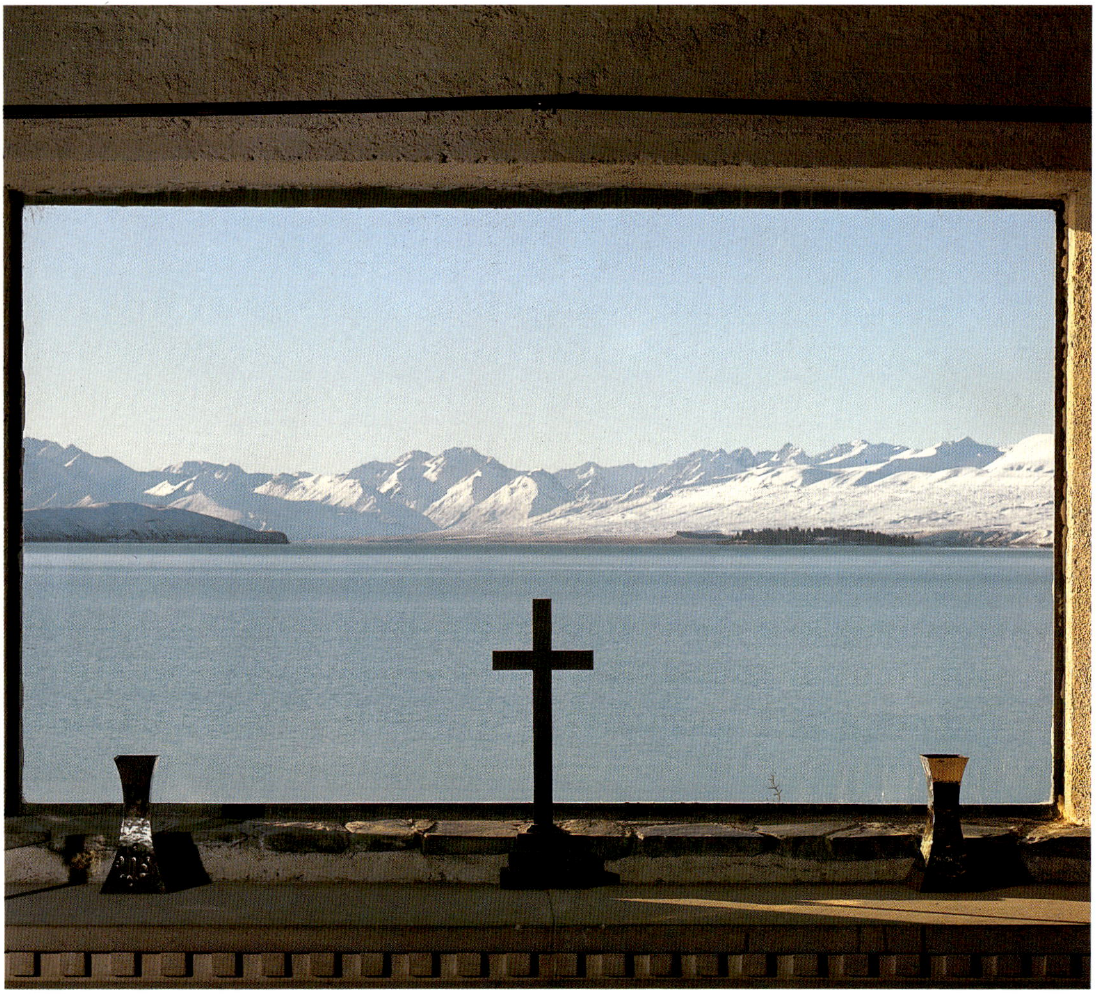

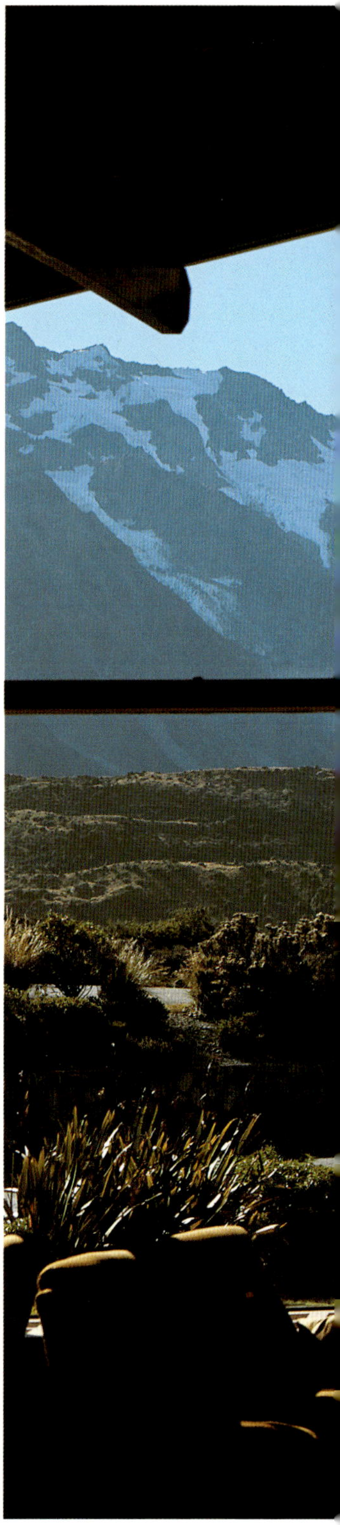

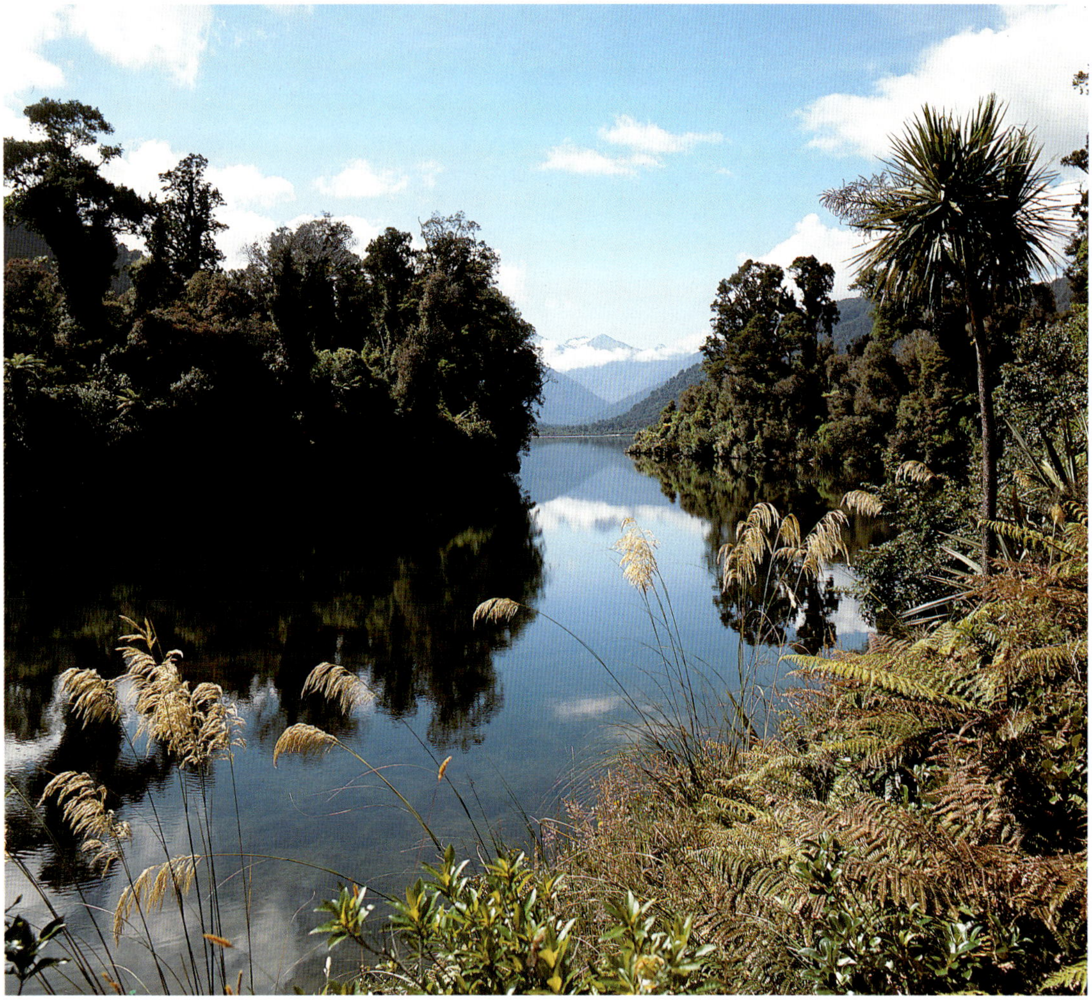

Left Above
The altar of the Church of the Good Shepherd, Tekapo, looking toward the head of the lake. The little stone church is a joy to enter, but the view from the altar window an experience.

Left Below
Lake Moeraki is in South Westland, just north of Haast Pass. The excellent fishing lakes to be found here have dense rainforest right to the water's edge. The graceful kotuku (white heron) is often seen on the shores of Lake Moeraki as its nesting place is 100km north, on the Okarito Lagoon.

Above
Another magnificent window view, this time from the Hermitage at Mount Cook village. Aoraki/Mount Cook is New Zealand's highest peak at 3754m and is the focal point of the Aoraki/Mount Cook National Park. Everywhere are incredible vistas, whether driving in along the shores of Lake Pukaki, on an alpine flight over the Southern Alps, or skiing down the Tasman Glacier.

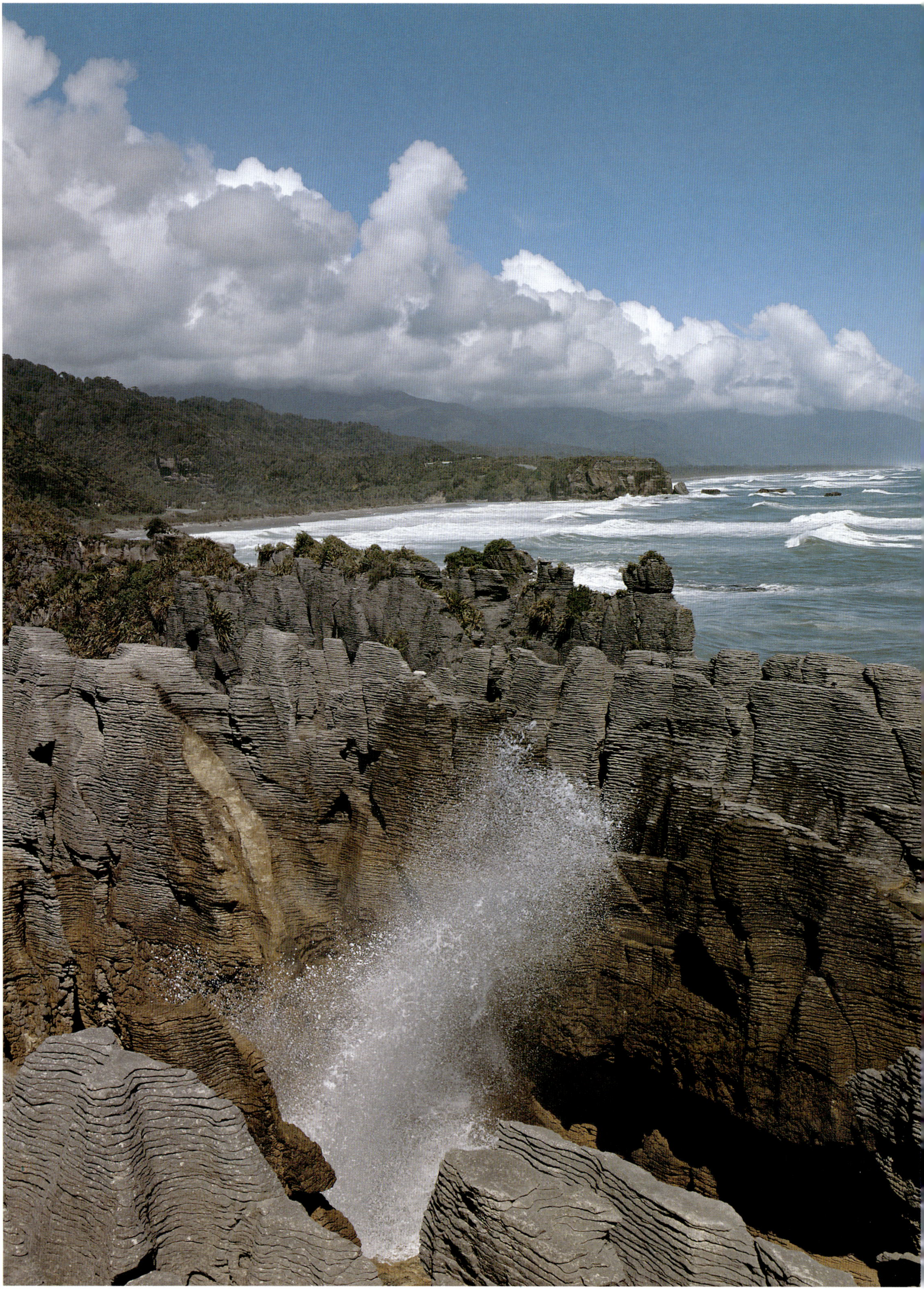

Left
Stormy surf rushing in from the Tasman Sea has carved pancake rock formations on the limestone headland at Punakaiki. The sea swirls into large cavernous holes, sending jet spray high into the air.

Above
Franz Josef and Fox Glaciers are accessible from the main highway in South Westland and guided walks or scenic flights can be arranged from either township. Franz Josef (above) is said to be a river of tears, wept by Hine at the death of her beloved Wawa.

Right Above
Generally speaking the eastern coastline of the South Island has long sweeping beaches, with the occasional rock headland. The City and Port of Timaru serves the large farming community of South Canterbury. Caroline Bay is on Timaru's foreshore and draws many summer holidaymakers to its annual Christmas Carnival.

Above
The headwaters of the Waimakariri and Bealey Rivers are found deep in the Southern Alps in the Arthur's Pass National Park. Here they join to become one of several wide braided rivers that flow into the Canterbury Plains, the widest area of flat land in New Zealand.

Right
Ashburton is the commercial centre for the plains of Mid Canterbury, a farming area which runs to the foothills of the Southern Alps. It is strategically close to Mt Hutt ski area which has hosted the World Ski Cup.

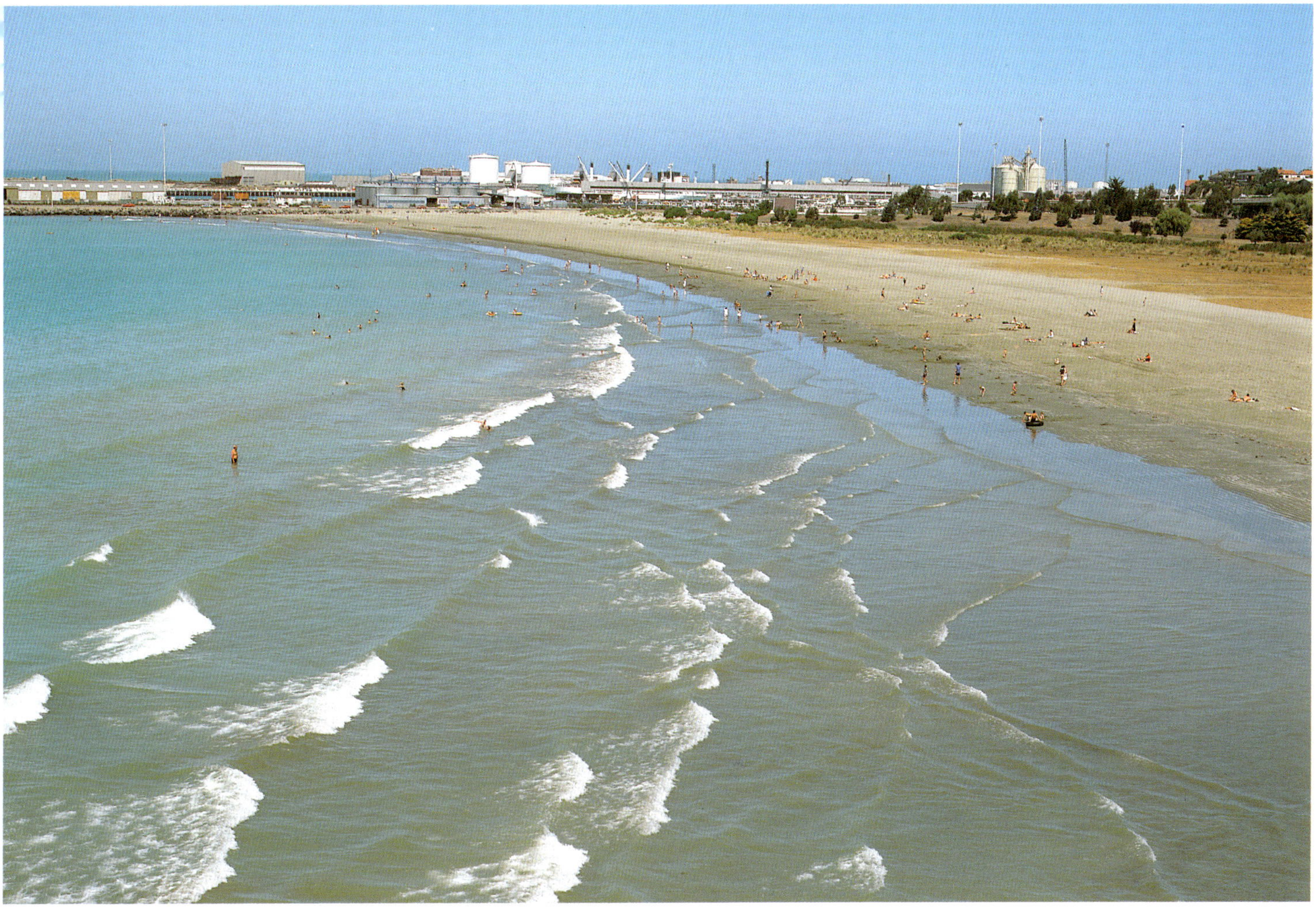

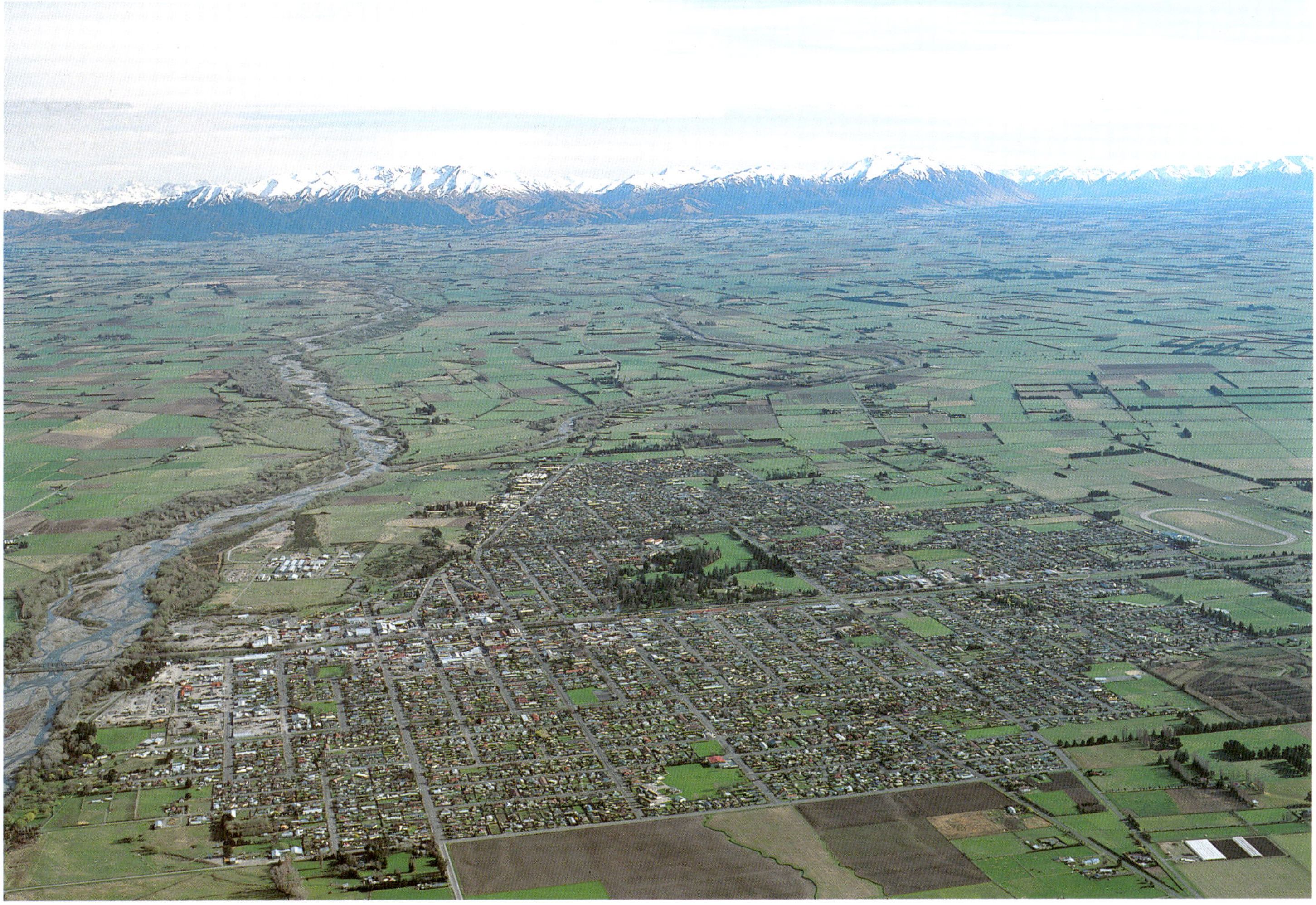

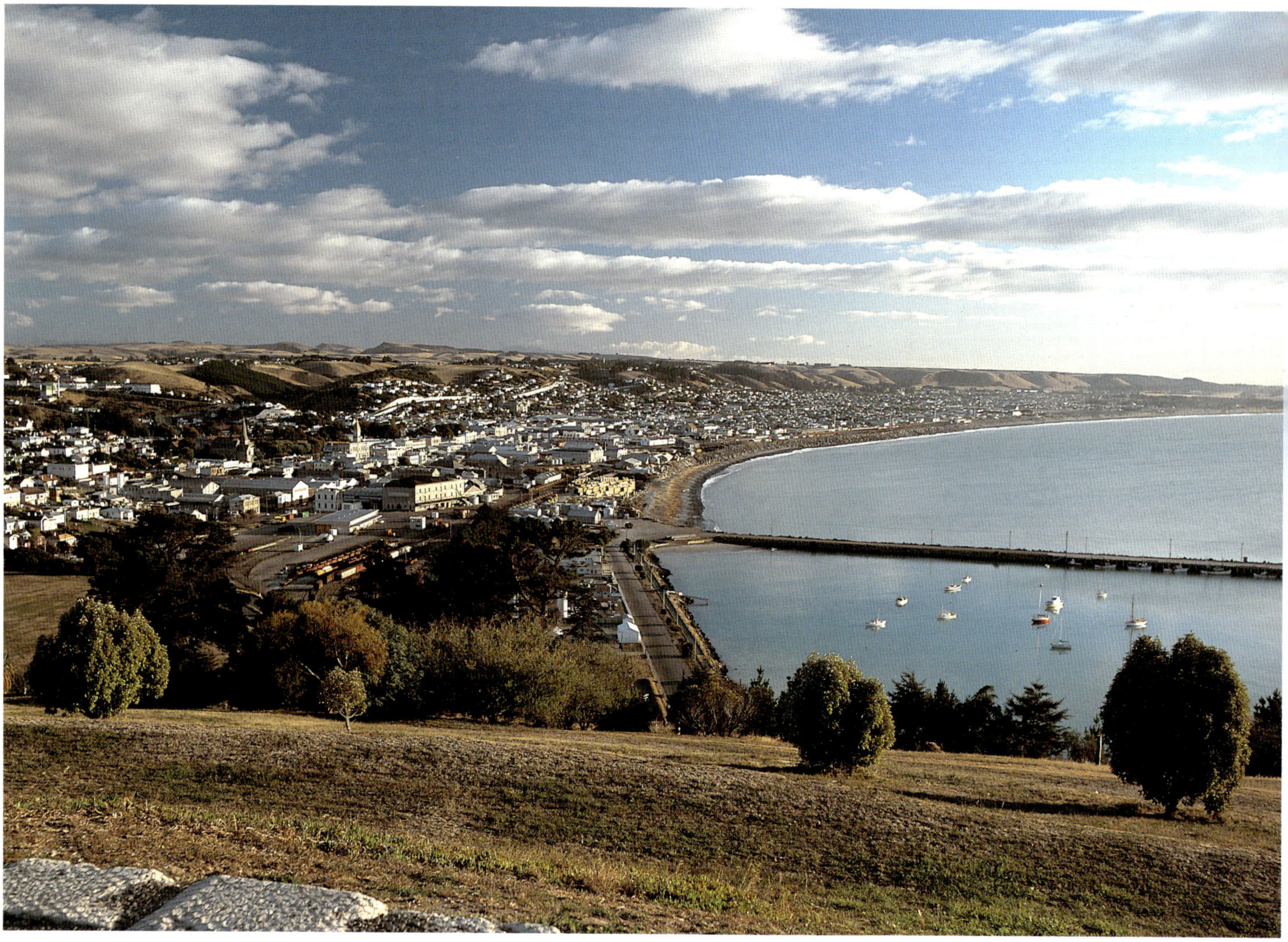

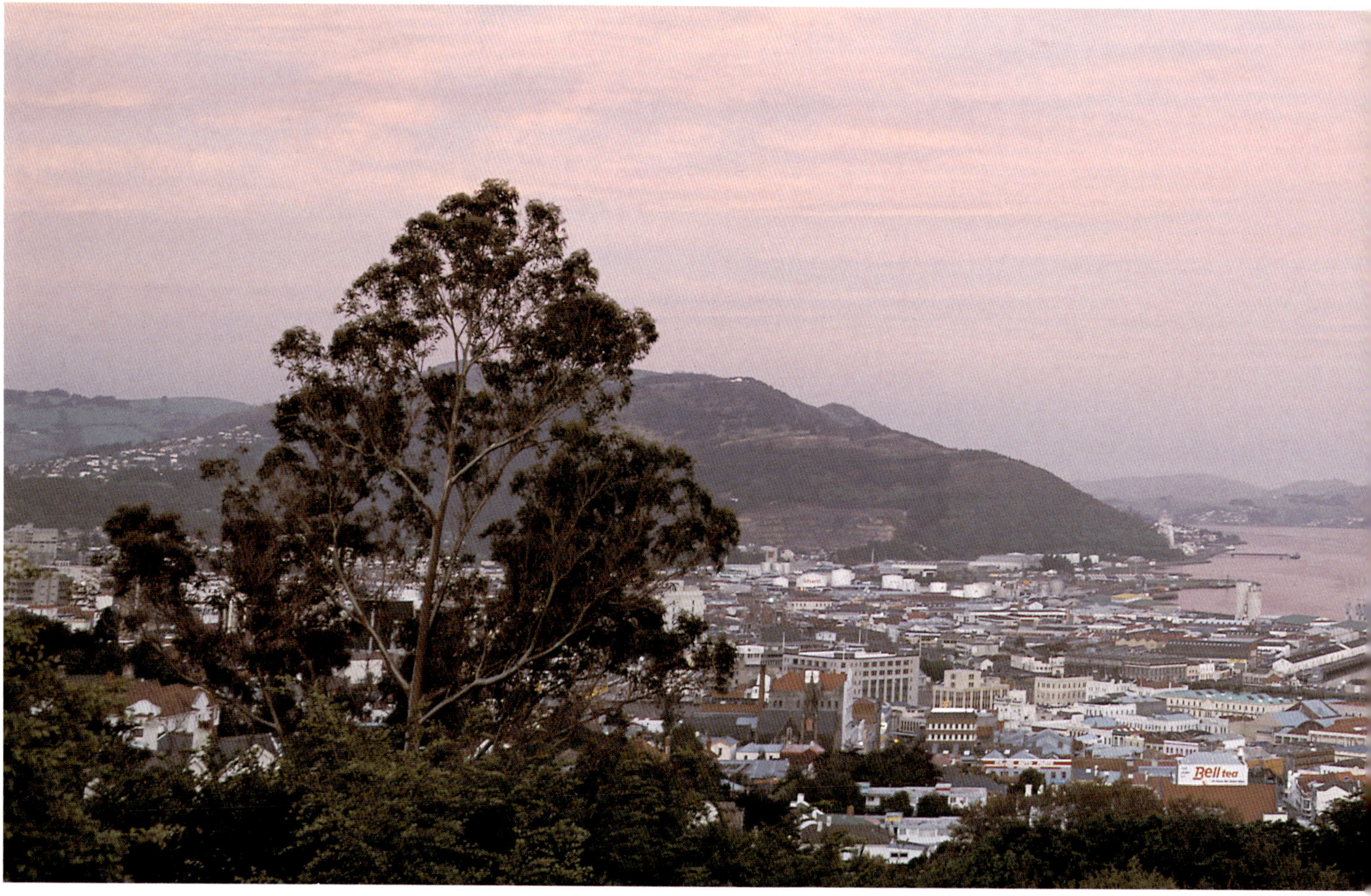
Bell tea

Left
This is a view of Oamaru city and port, the commercial centre of the rich farming and market gardening region of North Otago. If you look carefully you will be able to distinguish prominent buildings of the city that are constructed in the attractive cream Oamaru stone which is quarried from the surrounding hill-slopes.

Below
Dunedin is one of the most attractive cities of the South Island. Steep hill suburbs spread from the end of Otago Harbour, giving wonderful panoramas of harbour, peninsula and coast.

Right
Dunedin's settlers were Scottish and the city flourished after the discovery of gold in the province in 1861. Many fine Victorian homes and stone buildings are found throughout the city, the old buildings of Otago University being one of the best examples. This was New Zealand's first university, founded in 1869.

Above
Christchurch's city fathers were from England and the inner city radiates from a formal English Cathedral Square. Christchurch has traditionally been endowed with talented architects, and buildings old and new blend well along the banks of the Avon River which meanders through the central city.

Right Above
A favourite with visitors to Christchurch is the scenic drive over the Port Hills to Lyttelton Harbour, an extinct volcanic crater. From the Summit Road are interesting historic walkways. The 782 passengers off The First Four Ships that sailed up this harbour in 1850, took the Bridle Path to Christchurch to begin life in the Canterbury Association's new settlement.

Right Below
Christchurch is the largest city in the South Island, known as the "Garden City" because of its magnificent parks, reserves and home gardens. Victoria Square is a pleasant inner city meeting place on the banks of the Avon River.

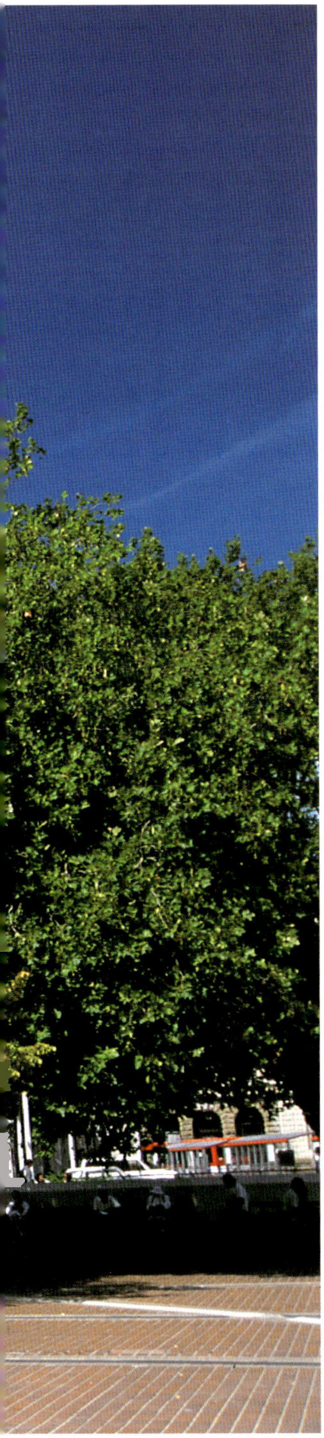

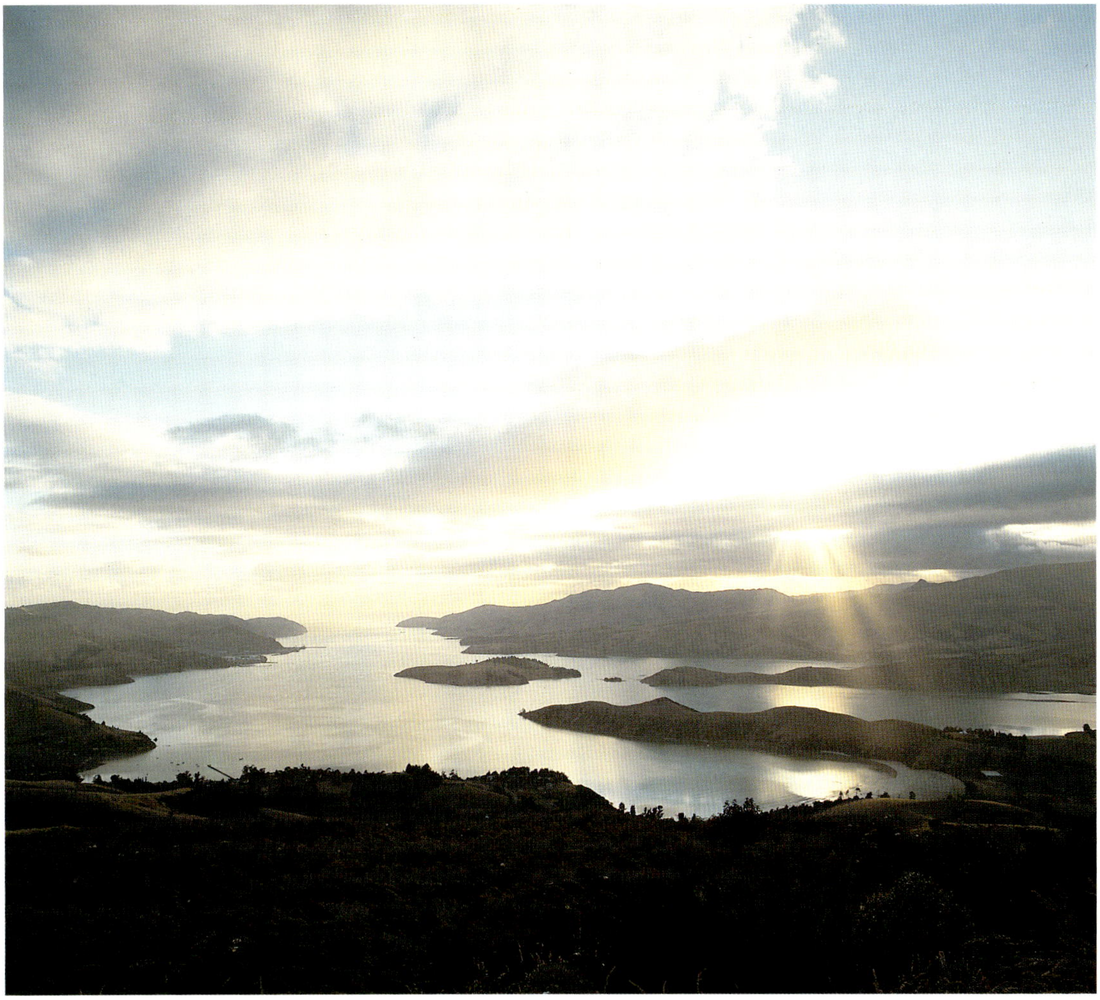

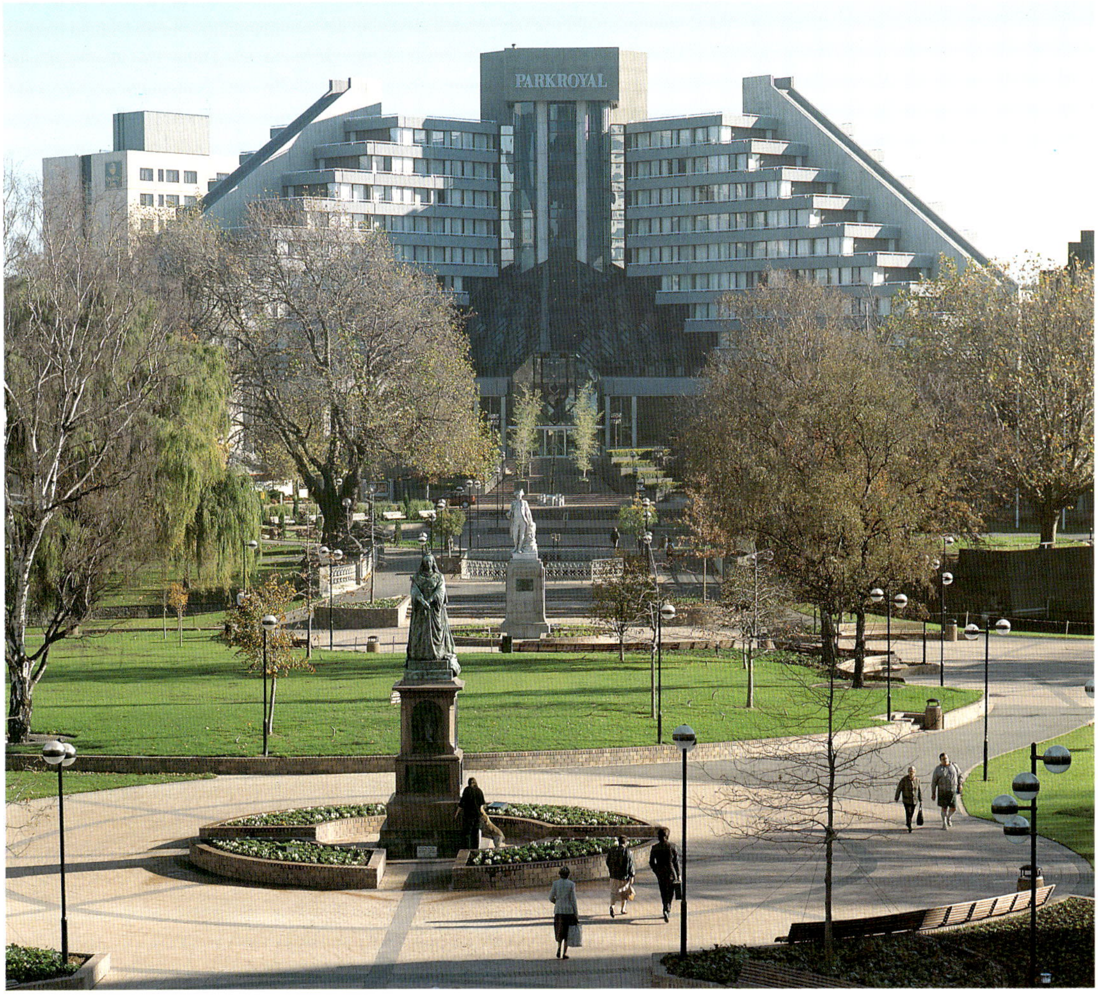
PARKROYAL

Below
Since its beginnings Canterbury's wealth has been in its grazing lands. Large sheep runs developed throughout the province, none more successfully than those in North Canterbury. These healthy Canterbury lambs are fattening on Leslie Hills Station near Hanmer.

Right
The Southern Alps, which run nearly the length of the South Island, completely dominate its geography and weather patterns. They also have a strong influence on the recreational pursuits of many of the population. Here in Christchurch for example, residents have several commercial or club skifields within easy driving distance.

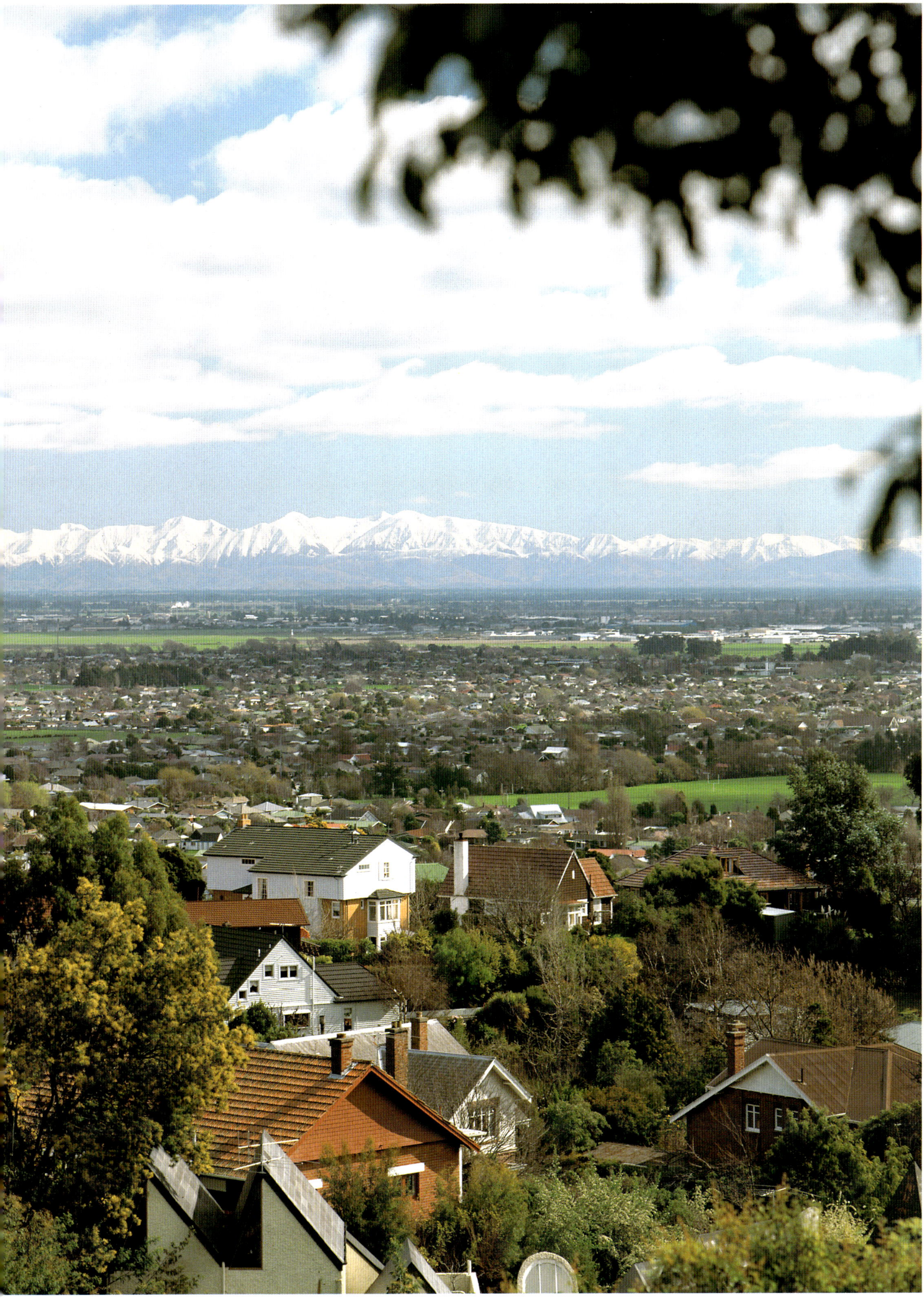

Above
The North Canterbury alpine village at Hanmer Springs is just across the Waiau River, fed from the eastern slopes of the Spenser Mountains. Surrounded by exotic forest, it is a delightful little resort. Hanmer's main attraction is its outdoor thermal spa baths which are especially enjoyable during winter when you can relax in the warmth, surrounded by snow-capped peaks or even with snow lightly falling around you.

Right
The township of Kaikoura, nestled under mountains bearing the same name, has become important to the tourist industry because of the whales that pass close to the shoreline. Small groups of tourists are taken offshore to see those amazing mammals rise for air and with a spectacular flick of their triangular tail, return to the depths of the ocean.

Left Below
For many Picton is departure point by ferry for the North Island, but for South Island boaties, it is just the beginning. Cruising amongst the Marlborough Sounds is a unique experience, whether in and out of bush clad inlets or remote farm headlands. The fishing is great and the scenery even better.